The Big Litt.
DAD JOKES

Compiled by Ben Manning

MONTPELIER PUBLISHING

ISBN: 9798360426226
Published in Great Britain by Montpelier Publishing.
Printed and distributed by Amazon KDP.
This edition © 2022. All rights reserved.

THE BIG LITTLE BOOK OF DAD JOKES

Generally speaking, my wife is generally speaking.

*

Why is the winner of Miss Universe always from Earth?

*

My father always used to say, 'when one door closes, another one opens.' He was a lovely man, but a terrible cabinet maker.

*

I hate Russian dolls. They're so full of themselves.

> **Serve it up and I'll try.**

> **Guess what's for dinner.**

I've decided to do something about my drinking, so this January I'm going dry. Dry sherry...dry martini...dry white wine...

*

Q. Name someone who is associated with misogyny.
A. Mr and Mrs Ogyny?

*

I don't trust Weight Watchers. When I looked at their website the first thing they asked was 'will you accept cookies'?

THE BIG LITTLE BOOK OF DAD JOKES

I found a wooden shoe in my toilet the other day. It was clogged.

> You shouldn't make fun of fat people. They have enough on their plates already.

*

A woman has the last word in any argument. Anything a man says after that is the beginning of a new argument.

*

A man noticed his hairline was receding slightly. 'Oh no!' he said to his wife. 'What if I'm going bald?' 'Don't worry,' said his wife, 'I read in a magazine that baldness is a sign of both intelligence and virility.' 'Oh no!' exclaimed the man again. 'What if I'm not going bald?!'

*

If Eve wore a leaf, what did Adam wear?
He wore a hole in it.

*

'I'd like to buy a pair of trousers please.'
'What leg?'
'Both of them'.

*

My wife hit the roof when she found out I'd replaced our bed with a trampoline.

*

THE BIG LITTLE BOOK OF DAD JOKES

'How much is this handkerchief?'
'Ten pounds'.
'That's far too much money to blow on something.'

*

McGregor: Have ye forgotten about that five pounds I lent ye?
McNab: Not yet, man, but I'm workin' on it.

*

On the train home, I enjoy a crossword. 'Get out of my way', 'move your briefcase' and 'turn your music down' are some of my favourites.

*

'See that man over there? He once cheated me out of a fortune'.
'How did he do that?'
'He wouldn't let me marry his daughter'.

How do you help a cannibal?

Give him a hand.

I went for a medical check up and the doctor said, 'Don't eat anything fatty'. I asked him 'what about bacon?' 'Didn't you understand what I said?' replied the doctor. 'I said don't eat anything - Fatty!'

*

Husband: Am I the only one you have ever been with?
Wife: Oh yes! All the others were nines or tens.

*

THE BIG LITTLE BOOK OF DAD JOKES

> **This house believes we should abolish democracy. All those in favour, raise your hand.**

I accidentally handed my wife a gluestick instead of her chapstick. She still isn't talking to me.

*

Railway station announcement: Will the person who lost a crate of whisky this morning platform 9, please go to the lost property office, where the man who found it has just been handed in.

*

My boss told me to have a good day. So I went home.

*

A man was lying in bed looking at his wife. 'Looking at you makes me think of the National Lottery,' he said. 'Why?' asked the wife. 'Am I worth millions to you?' 'No,' replied the husband. 'I wish you'd roll over.'

*

The inventor of autocorrect died recently.
I didn't even know he was I'll.

*

The older I get, the better I was.

THE BIG LITTLE BOOK OF DAD JOKES

My body is a temple. Ancient and crumbling.

*

I went to that Reading Festival recently. How are people supposed to concentrate on their books with all that loud music going on?

*

I was at the DIY store the other day and the assistant asked if I wanted decking. Fortunately I managed to get the first punch in.

*

An old woman phoned the police and told them that the man three doors down was sunbathing nude in his garden. When asked by the police how she knew, she replied 'If I stand on my bedroom windowsill, hang onto the gutter and pull myself up, I can see it all.'

*

'My wife and I went to Spain for our wedding ceremony.'
'Seville?'
'No, we had a church service.'

You don't seem as well dressed as you were when we were married 40 years ago.

I don't see why not. I'm still wearing the same suit.

THE BIG LITTLE BOOK OF DAD JOKES

"How did you find the steak, sir?"

"It was hiding under the lettuce!"

The grass may be greener on the other side of the fence, but at least you don't have to mow it.

*

McTavish: Let me pour ye another. I've heard ye like good whisky.
McNab: That I do - but pour me another one anyway.

*

You can always tell who the glue-sniffers are in your area. They all stick together.

*

'Steward, how dare you enter my cabin without knocking? What if you had come in while I was undressed!'
'Impossible, madam'.
'Why?'
'Because I always look through the keyhole first'.

*

I've been trying to find my mother-in-law's killer for five years. But no-one will agree to do it!

*

I started my puncture repair business from a small flat.

*

THE BIG LITTLE BOOK OF DAD JOKES

I often get letters marked 'final demand'. But it never is – if anything, they keep asking for even more money!

*

Whatever you do in life, always give one hundred percent. Unless you're giving blood.

*

I asked my dentist if he could suggest anything for yellow teeth and he said 'how about a brown tie?'

*

Five out of six people agree that Russian Roulette is safe.

*

Tramp: Spare some change for a piece of cake, lady?
Lady: Surely bread is good enough for you?
Tramp: Normally it would be, but today's my birthday.

*

Three's Company

A 90 year old man married a 25 year old woman but after a few months she failed to get pregnant so the gentleman visited his doctor.

'My wife is desperate to have a child, doctor; what do you suggest?' asked the man.

The medical man, not wanting to upset the man by telling him he was too old to father a child, said 'perhaps you should consider getting a young lodger to live with you, and see what happens'.

Six months later the man returned. 'Doctor,' he said, 'my wife is now pregnant'. 'Congratulations', said the doctor. 'Did you take my advice about getting a young lodger?' 'Yes,' replied the man. 'And now she's pregnant as well!'

A debt collector is the most popular man in town - people he visits are always telling him to come back next week.

*

THE BIG LITTLE BOOK OF DAD JOKES

I just Googled 'cigarette lighter' and got 1,000 matches.

*

I felt so depressed that I went out and bought 500 paracetamol tablets. The problem is, I can't get the wife to take them.

*

I answered an advertisement in the paper for a 'Colour portrait of the Queen with brass wall hanger' for £39.99 and all I got was a postage stamp and a drawing pin.

*

'Dad, can you put my shoes on?' 'No son, I don't think they'll fit me'.

I keep reading in the newspaper that smoking is bad for me. So I've made a decision. I'm going to give up reading.

I don't know why dairy farmers are always moaning about the cost of milk. They've got a field full of cows they can get it from for free!

*

I'm not saying my local pub is rough, but on quiz night the first question was 'what are you looking at?'

*

THE BIG LITTLE BOOK OF DAD JOKES

My granddad never recovered from having his wheelchair oiled.
After that, he went downhill fast.

*

Did you hear about the man who died after drinking furniture polish?
He had a terrible end, but a lovely finish.

*

Due to the success of my bonsai tree business, I am very pleased to announce we will be shortly moving to smaller premises.

*

What do you call a magician who's lost his magic?
Ian.

On Valentine's Day I booked a table for me and my new girlfriend. Turns out she doesn't even like snooker.

*

My wife said 'you never take me anywhere expensive.' So I drove her to the petrol station.

*

'Did she marry that footballer for his money?'
'No, that's what she divorced him for.'

*

My wife wanted to put the magic back into our marriage. So I put her in a wardrobe and made her disappear.

Whoever said 'diamonds are forever' has never heard of Cash Converters.

*

Gifted Child

My son is three years old and yesterday I took him shopping. When we got home, he had a chocolate bar in his pocket. Now, I didn't buy it and he certainly didn't buy it, so I marched him straight back to the shopping centre - and this time took him to the jewellers.

'Why don't you kiss me like George Clooney,' said an amorous wife as she left the cinema. 'Don't be ridiculous,' replied her husband. 'Have you any idea how much he gets paid to do that?'

*

There's a nudist convention in our town next week. I might go if I've got nothing on.

*

Then there was the secretary who was unsure whether to end a letter with 'yours faithfully' or 'yours sincerely', so she put 'yours sinfully'.

*

How many Anglicans does it take to change a light bulb?
My grandfather donated that lightbulb to the church and you'll change it over my dead body!

*

'I'm not a sexist,' announced the company director. 'All my staff are paid equally – and I even let the women work longer hours than the men in order to make sure they can earn it.'

*

The reward for a job well done is more work.

*

Magistrate: You have been appearing before me in this court with depressing regularity for over ten years.
Defendant: Can I help it if you don't get promoted?

*

My wife and I often laugh about how competitive we are with each other. But I laugh louder.

*

A book fell on my head the other day. I have only my shelf to blame.

*

Sign in an optician's shop: 'If you do not see what you want in the window, you have come to the right place'.

*

Then there was the man who left his job at the tiddlywinks factory, because it was counterproductive.

*

I have the body of a god. Unfortunately, it's Buddha.

*

THE BIG LITTLE BOOK OF DAD JOKES

I've got a lovely step ladder. I never knew my real ladder.

*

I went to a posh school. In fact it was so posh, our gym was called James.

*

I decided to sell all my old voyeurism tapes on Ebay. No bids so far, but there are 17 watchers.

*

If evolution is the survival of the fittest, is sumo wrestling the survival of the fattest?

*

A vicar was alarmed to find his wife rummaging through the church collection after morning service. 'It's alright dear,' she said, noting the look of concern on his face. 'I was just looking for a button to sew on your cassock.'

*

The worst part about working in a Job Centre is even if you get fired, you still have to turn up the next day.

*

I recently sold my vacuum cleaner. Well, it was only collecting dust.

*

Beauty is in the eye of the beer holder...

A wife looked at the bank statement for her and her husband's joint account.
'You spent £100 this month on beer!' she cried in horror.
'You spent the same on makeup!' said the husband, pointing to the statement.
'Darling,' replied the wife, 'that was to make me look beautiful for you.'
'Well that's what the beer was for as well!' replied the husband.

They say 'getting there is half the fun'. Unless you're travelling by Ryan Air.

*

My wife's just told me she's broken her satnav and wants me to buy a new one. Well she can get lost!

*

When my boyfriend told me he worked in the lion's enclosure at the zoo, I knew he was a keeper.

*

My wife says I'm spontaneous. How the hell would she know - I've only known her for three days.

My wife's decided that from now on we should sleep in separate bedrooms. That's fine by me. I've chosen that blonde's bedroom at number 23.

*

One problem with growing older is that it becomes progressively more difficult to find a famous historical figure who hadn't achieved much by your age.

*

What do you call a woman who knows where her husband is every night? A widow.

*

A university student delivered a pizza to an old woman's house. 'I suppose you want a tip?' said the old woman. 'That would be great,' said the student, 'but the other guy who does deliveries told me not to expect too much - he said if I got 50p, I'd be lucky.' The old woman looked hurt. 'Well, to prove him wrong,' she said, 'here's five pounds. What are you studying?' 'Applied psychology,' replies the student.

*

Marriage is all about compromise. The husband admits he's wrong, and the wife agrees with him.

'The food here is terrible, isn't it?'

'Yes, and the portions are so small!'

A tip for the barber

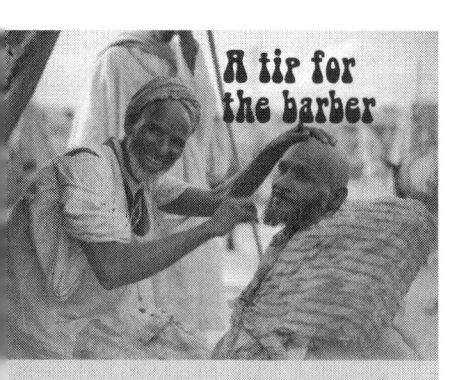

A man came into a barber's shop in a small town and said 'how long do I have to wait? The barber looked at the line of customers and said 'about two hours'.
The man left the shop, but didn't come back. The next day, the man came back and asked the barber again, 'how long do I have to wait?' Again, the barber looked at the queue and said, 'about two hours.' Once more, the man disappeared, and didn't come back.
The next day, the same thing happened all over again. The barber looked at one of his regular customers and said, 'Every day he comes in and asks how long he has to wait, but then he disappears. Where does he go?' The regular customer paused for a moment, then sighed and said, 'to your wife.'

A teenage girl said to her mother,
'Mum, I've started dating Fred next door.'
'But he's old - he could be your father.'
'Age is just a number, mum'.
'No dear...that's not what I meant. I meant he actually **could** be your father'.

*

I'm not saying my wife's fat, but I've had to put all the chocolate biscuits somewhere she can't reach them. On the floor.

*

A woman nearly drowned at the seaside, and a lifeguard gave her the kiss of life on the beach.
'What are you doing, man?' demanded her husband.
'Artificial respiration,' said the lifeguard.
'Well for heaven's sake stop messing around and give her the real thing!' replied the man.

*

THE BIG LITTLE BOOK OF DAD JOKES

Did you hear about the man who tried to eat four crackers in a minute?
He choked on one of the paper hats.

*

If you don't pay your TV licence, you could get sent to prison. Where you can watch TV all day, without needing a licence.

*

Husband: I made a new discovery at work today, darling.
Wife: You've been employed by Land Rover for a year now, darling. Couldn't you try a new joke?

*

Woman (to dentist): I don't know which is worse, having a tooth pulled, or having a baby.
Dentist: Well make your mind up, I've got to adjust the chair!

*

I once had a racing snail, and in order to make it faster I removed its shell. If anything, it made it more sluggish.

*

I'm delighted with my wife's new diet. She's lost four pounds in five days. I've worked out that in three months' time, she'll have disappeared completely.

*

'That's a fancy looking golf ball. What's that little flashing light on it for?'
'So it can show you where it is in the bushes.'
'What's that little hatch on the bottom for?'
'If it gets buried in a bunker, a little shovel comes out and digs it up for you.'

'What are those two bits on the side for?'
'If it goes in the water, two little paddles come out and it swims back to you.'
'That's amazing! Where on earth did you get it?'
'I found it.'

*

For sale: clock with half a face. For a limited time only.

*

I once got kidnapped by a gang of mime artists. They did unspeakable things to me.

*

That joke's so old, the first time I heard that joke I laughed so much I dribbled down my bib.

*

I was a teetotaller for twenty years…but when I turned 21….oh boy!

*

Officer (inspecting recruit): Your boots are dirty. Haven't you cleaned them?
Recruit: No.
Officer: No what?!
Recruit: No polish.

*

I'm going to miss my mother in law this Christmas, but I know she'll be up there looking down on us all…moaning at us because we won't mend the stairlift.

THE BIG LITTLE BOOK OF DAD JOKES

Where do lobsters catch trains in London?
King's Crustacean.

*

If life begins at 40, what ended at 39?

*

At what age is it appropriate to tell my dog that he's adopted?

*

'I had to leave the army, I had problems with my arms and legs.'
'Why, what was wrong with them?'
'My arms kept going up and my legs kept walking backwards'.

*

A drum and a cymbal fell over a cliff. Badoom, tish!

*

Did you hear? Old Mr Jones dropped dead, just five days after getting married again.

Ah well. At least he didn't suffer much!

What do you get if you cross a Swedish pop group with Fred Flintstone? Abba-dabba doo!

*

A woodworm walks in to a pub and asks 'where is the bar tender?'

*

Why do fifty pence pieces have straight sides?
So they can be removed from a Scotsman's hand with a spanner.

*

I used to go out with an archaeologist,
but she kept digging up the past.

*

I don't make predictions, and I never will.

*

My wife told me 'sex is better on holiday'. That was one postcard I wasn't happy to receive.

*

We had an inch of snow yesterday so I did some panic-buying in the shops. I bought the same things as I usually do, I just screamed loudly while doing it.

*

Did you hear about the Italian selling fake sausage?
Turns out it was a false salami.

*

Age is just a (large) number

A man's wife had just bought a new line of expensive cosmetics guaranteed to make her look years younger. She sat in front of the mirror for what had to be hours, applying the 'miracle' products.

Finally, when she was done, she turned to her husband and asked, 'Darling, honestly now, what age would you say I am?' He nodded his head in assessment, and carefully said, 'Well, judging from your skin, twenty. Your hair, eighteen. Your figure, twenty-five.'

'Oh, you're so sweet!' gushed the wife. 'Hang on,' he replied. 'I'm not finished adding it up yet.'

My wife told me to stop impersonating a flamingo.
I had to put my foot down.

*

The worst thing about dating a blind woman is having to get her husband's voice exactly right.

*

Don't you just hate it when people answer their own questions?
I do.

*

Undertakers make the best friends
- they're the last ones to let you down.

*

THE BIG LITTLE BOOK OF DAD JOKES

Why is that smoking will kill you, and bacon will kill you, but smoking bacon will cure it?

*

Did you hear about the man who did a PhD on the life of Walt Disney? He ended up with a Mickey Mouse degree.

*

Where there's a will, there's a relative.

*

'Pass me that shovel.'
'That snow shovel?'
'What do you mean, of course it is!'

*

'I can't remember what the doctor said I'm suffering from – it's on the tip of my tongue.'
'Mouth ulcers?'

*

Since I removed all my car mirrors, I've never looked back.

The easiest way to scare your husband is to ask him if he knows what today is.

*

I can't wait to try out that new machine in the gym.
It's got coke, crisps, chocolate, everything.

THE BIG LITTLE BOOK OF DAD JOKES

I don't like political jokes. Too many of them get elected.

*

Newsflash: In Birmingham, 50,000 tiles have gone missing from the Scrabble factory. Police say they suspect vowel play.

*

Dr Smith: That new nurse kept putting the oral thermometers in the wrong place.
Dr Jones: Rectum?
Dr Smith: Well it didn't do them much good!

*

I drink to forget, but I can't remember what!

*

The doctor told me he had some news that was going to be hard for me to hear. He said 'you're going deaf.'

THE BIG LITTLE BOOK OF DAD JOKES

The wife told me she was going to get a tattoo. I came home to find the front garden full of bagpipers.

*

Hitchhiker (to motorist): Thanks for picking me up. But how do you know I'm not a serial killer?
Motorist: Come now! Two serial killers in the same car – what are the chances of that?

*

I stopped the garage the other day to get my tyres pumped up. I couldn't believe it cost £1 – still, that's inflation for you!

*

'Do you have a disabled toilet?'
'No, it's working perfectly.'

*

Then there was the actor who bought a corduroy pillow so that he could always make headlines.

*

To the mathematician who invented the zero - thanks for nothing!

*

A man cancelled having his tonsils removed, after seeing a sign in the ward that said 'Beware – thieves operate in this hospital'.

*

Whenever I have a row with my wife, I always make sure to get the last word in. Usually it's 'yes, dear...'

*

THE BIG LITTLE BOOK OF DAD JOKES

> Last week I washed the car with my son. He said 'Dad, can't you use a sponge instead?'

The grass is always greener on the other side of the fence. Usually because it's growing on a big heap of manure.

*

Light travels faster than sound. This is why some people appear bright until you hear them speak.

*

I can never seem to drink enough beer. No matter how much I have, I've still always got a raging thirst when I wake up.

*

A Scotsman, while attempting to pick up a penny from the middle of Oxford Street, was run over and killed by a bus. The coroner's verdict was 'death by natural causes'.

My Esperanto lessons are going well.
I can almost speak it like a native now.

*

Late one night Jones heard a knock at the door. He opened it and saw a policeman standing there holding up a photograph of a woman. 'is this your wife, sir?' asked the constable. 'Yes,' replied Jones. 'I'm afraid it looks as if she's been in a bad accident' said the policeman. 'I know,' said Jones, 'but she was much prettier when she was younger.'

*

The other day my new dog attacked my wife, so I decided enough was enough. If anyone is willing to give her a good home, her name's Maureen, she's 47 and a good cook.

*

'I've just had a very trying evening with my wife.'
'How many times did you try?'

*

Money doesn't go as far as it used to, but it makes up for it by going faster.

*

I asked my wife what she wanted for Christmas and she told me 'nothing would make me happier than a diamond necklace,' so I bought her nothing.

*

Two TV aerials met on a roof and got married. The ceremony wasn't much good but the reception was excellent.

*

To be frank...I'd have to change my name.

THE BIG LITTLE BOOK OF DAD JOKES

A wee Scottish lad was speaking to his father. 'Dad, ye promised me a poond if I was top o' the class. We'll I've been top all week!' His father handed over the money. 'Here ye are,' he said, 'but dinnae study so hard. It's no good for ye!'

*

John Lennon: I'm having an affair with another woman.
Mrs Lennon: Oh no!
John Lennon: How did you guess?

Have you read Marx?

Yes, I think it's those wicker beach chairs.

*

'I've come about the handyman job'.
'Can you lay bricks?'
'No.'
'Can you plaster?'
'No.'
'Can you do any carpentry?'
'No.'
'Then what's handy about you?'
'I only live round the corner.'

*

Sign on Scottish road: Diversion: toll bridge ahead.

*

My granny is always forgetting where she left her glasses. So I told her just drink out of the bottle instead.

*

Then there was the dumb blonde who used toothpaste as a douche, because the packet said 'reduces cavities by up to 50%'.

*

Most people are shocked when they find out how incompetent I am as an electrician.

*

An archaeologist is the only person who is happy that his career lies in ruins.

*

The Austrians are clever. They've managed to convince the world that Hitler was German and Mozart was Austrian.

*

I tried to remarry my ex-wife, but she found out I was only after her for my money.

*

The Queen was visiting a hospital ward and spoke to a woman who had just given birth to her twelfth child. 'After fathering that many children your husband should have a knighthood' said Her Majesty. The woman replied 'He's already got one Ma'am, but he won't wear it.'

*

The best thing about being divorced is you get to sleep around. You can sleep on the left of the bed, the right of the bed, the middle of the bed...

*

Why is an astronomer always happy?
Because his business is looking up.

*

Some salesman tried to get me to take out a funeral plan. I said 'that's the last thing I'll need.'

*

Heredity: something a father believes in until his son starts acting like a fool.

*

Another 'world's oldest man' has died. This is beginning to look suspicious.

*

The man who invented human cloning died last week. His relatives were beside themselves with grief.

*

What are the best Christmas lights you will ever see?
The red ones on the back of your mother-in-law's car when she finally leaves.

*

'Doctor, I keep seeing spots before my eyes.'
'Have you seen an opthalmologist?'
'No, just spots.'

*

My wife said she wanted some peace and quiet in the kitchen while she cooked - so I took the batteries out of the smoke alarm.

THE BIG LITTLE BOOK OF DAD JOKES

Dentist: Do you want helium?
Patient: Will it numb the pain?
Dentist: No, but it makes it quite funny when you scream.

*

Shinbone: a device for locating furniture in a darkened room.

*

I've just found out I'm colourblind. The diagnosis came right out of the purple.

*

My garage tends to charge a lot for parts. The other day I had to pay £200 for something called a 'long weight'.

*

So what if I don't know what 'Armageddon' means.
It's not the end of the world!

Do you have reservations?

Yes, but we came anyway.

THE BIG LITTLE BOOK OF DAD JOKES

How do you make an elephant fly?
First, you'll need a three foot long zip...

*

'Life is a journey, not a destination' - the new motto of British Rail.

*

Q. What do you find on pool tables, as well as in men's trousers?
A. Pockets.

*

'My boyfriend proposed to me last night, and now we're not speaking'.
'Why not?'
'You should have heard what he proposed!'

*

My wife and I tried out a new position last night.
I stood at the sink and she lay on the sofa.

*

Doctor: Have you been limiting your alcohol consumption to two pints of beer a day like I told you?
Patient: Yes doctor.
Doctor: Then I don't understand why your condition hasn't improved.
Patient: Perhaps it's because before I took your advice, I only drank one pint of beer a day?

*

Girl (to golf caddy): I've just been stung by a bee!
Caddy: Where?
Girl: Between the first and second hole.
Caddy: Try narrowing your stance a bit.

THE BIG LITTLE BOOK OF DAD JOKES

Hotel guest: How much is the room?
Manager: £300 a night sir.
Hotel guest: That's a bit steep.
Manager: We'll throw in breakfast as well.
Hotel guest: For £300 I'll want it brought in on a tray!

*

She: Darling, today is Valentine's Day. What are we doing?
He: Do you like France?
She: Oh yes!
He: And do you like Italy?
She: Oh yes, darling, yes!
He: Good. Because Italy is playing France at rugby tonight and it's on TV.

Speech bubbles:
- I'd like a deodorant for my husband.
- Certainly Madam. Ball type?
- No it's for his armpits.

*

I'm living proof that it's possible to be in love with the same woman after ten years of marriage. I just hope my wife doesn't find out about her.

*

Did you hear about the kidnapping at the school?
It's OK, he woke up.

*

Man (in lingerie shop): I'd like to buy a bra for my wife.
Assistant: Certainly sir. What size?

THE BIG LITTLE BOOK OF DAD JOKES

Man: Seven and three eighths.
Assistant: Bras don't come in that size. Are you sure?
Man: Positive!
Assistant: How did you measure her?
Man: I used my hat!

*

Remember to say to your wife every day those three little words that women love to hear: 'You are right'.

*

McTavish: I thought ye'd broken off yer engagement tae Maggie?
McNab: Aye, I did - but then I found she couldn't get the ring off!

*

Smith: I've had to remortgage the house to send my son to college. But all he does is lie in bed all day, drink, and chase women.
Jones: So you regret it?
Smith: Yes. I wish I'd gone myself!

*

If your wife wants to learn to drive, don't stand in her way.

Notice in church magazine: 'the meeting will be gin with prayer'.

*

Man (in chemist's shop) I'd like three condoms please miss!
Female assistant: (curtly) Don't 'miss' me!

THE BIG LITTLE BOOK OF DAD JOKES

Man: Alright then, I'd like four condoms!

*

I'd love a job making mirrors.
It's just something I could see myself doing.

*

Many a woman who appears to be throwing herself at a man is actually taking very careful aim.

*

A place for everything and everything in its place, they say. In my house, it's on the floor.

*

My job is secure. No-one else wants it.

*

Policeman (to drunk): Where do you think you're going?
Drunk: 'S'alright offisher, I'm going to a temperance lecture.
Policeman: Oh yes, and who's giving it?
Drunk: My wife.

*

A man went into a newsagent's and bought a paper. 'Would you like tomorrow's paper as well, sir?' asked the newsagent. 'How on earth can you sell me tomorrow's paper?' asked the man in a puzzled voice. 'Simple sir,' replied the newsagent. 'Just come back tomorrow'.

*

'When you were in Rome, did you do as the Romans do?'
'No, my wife was with me.'

Hugh Hefner was feeling poorly so he called the doctor. 'You'll have to have complete rest,' said the physician after examining him. 'I recommend you stay out of bed for two weeks.'

*

Marriage is when a man and woman become one. The trouble starts when they try to decide which one.

*

A drunk fancied a visit to a local house of ill-repute, but he got the addresses mixed up and went into a chiropodist's by mistake. 'Just wait in there and I'll be with you in a minute,' said the attractive receptionist. The drunk took all his clothes off and lay down on the couch. The receptionist walked in and said 'Good heavens, I was only expecting a foot!' The drunk winked and said 'come on darling, let's not quibble over a couple of inches!'

*

I may be old but I'll never be over the hill. Certainly not as long as I've got a car with a 998 cc engine.

*

Then there was the Irish priest who drank so much whisky that he thought VAT 69 was the Pope's telephone number.

*

My girlfriend refuses to have sex with me on religious grounds. So I've stopped taking her to the cemetery.

*

Definition of a cocaine dealer: someone who goes around sticking his business into other peoples' noses.

*

THE BIG LITTLE BOOK OF DAD JOKES

I asked my wife what she wanted for her birthday. 'Can I have a bookmark?' she said. You'd think after twenty years of marriage she'd remember my name is Brian.

*

'I wish to return these stockings.'
'Certainly madam. Did they not come up to your expectations?'
'No, they barely came up to my knees.'

*

I admire that blind prostitute - you've really got to hand it to her.

*

I've just burned 2000 calories. That's the last time I leave a cake in the oven while I have a nap.

*

A Scotsman arrived for his first day on a new job.
'Who are you?' said the foreman.
'I'm fine,' replied the Scotsman. And hoo's yersel?'

*

Two old gentlemen sat on a park bench discussing old friends who had died.
'It's Jones I miss the most,' sighed one.
'Why so?'
'I married his widow'.

*

Two Scotsmen were shipwrecked on a desert island with no food nor hope of rescue. 'Things couldnae get much worse', said McNab. 'Aye they could,' replied McTavish. 'I could hae bought a return ticket'.

I've just been fired from my job as a set designer. I left without making a scene.

*

Mrs Smith: My goodness, Mrs Jones. It must be ten years since I saw you. You look much older.
Mrs Jones: Really? Well I wouldn't have recognised you either if it wasn't for that coat!

*

Mark Anthony: I want to see Cleopatra immediately!
Servant: You can't, she's in bed with laryngitis.
Mark Anthony: Damn those Greeks!

*

He's the kind of man who will always go the extra mile. Usually to find a cheaper petrol station.

*

Last night my wife was complaining I never listen to her. Or something like that.

*

The man who invented Velcro has died. RIP.

*

My teachers told me I'd never amount to anything as I procrastinate too much. I told them 'just you wait!'

*

Other humour titles from Montpelier Publishing:

The Old Fashioned Joke Book
The Old Fashioned Joke Book 2
The Old Fashioned Joke Book 3
The Book of Church Jokes
After Dinner Laughs
After Dinner Laughs 2
Scottish Jokes
Large Print Jokes
Retirement Jokes
Welsh Jokes
Jewish Jokes
Medical Jokes
Non-Corny Knock Knock Jokes
Jokes for Kids
The Father Christmas Joke Book for Kids
Wedding Jokes
A Little Book of Limericks
Take my Wife! Hilarious Jokes of Love and Marriage

Order online now at Amazon!

THE BIG LITTLE BOOK OF DAD JOKES

Printed in Great Britain
by Amazon